IC COOKBOOK

MEGA BUNDLE – 2 Manuscripts in 1 – 80+ Interstitial Cystitis - friendly recipes including casseroles, roast, ice-cream and pie recipes

TABLE OF CONTENTS

Introduction

IC recipes for personal enjoyment but also for family enjoyment. You will love them for sure for how easy it is to prepare them.

ROASTED CUCUMBER

Serves: **3-4**
Prep Time: **10**   Minutes

Cook Time: **20**   Minutes

Total Time: **30**   Minutes

INGREDIENTS

- 2 lb. cucumber
- 2 tablespoons olive oil
- 1 tsp curry powder
- 1 tsp salt

DIRECTIONS

1. Preheat the oven to 400 F
2. Cut everything in half lengthwise
3. Toss everything with olive oil and place onto a prepared baking sheet
4. Roast for 18-20 minutes at 400 F or until golden brown
5. When ready remove from the oven and serve

Serves:	**3-4**	
Prep Time:	**10**	Minutes
Cook Time:	**20**	Minutes
Total Time:	**30**	Minutes

INGREDIENTS

- 2 delicata squashes
- 2 tablespoons olive oil
- 1 tsp curry powder
- 1 tsp salt

DIRECTIONS

1. Preheat the oven to 400 F
2. Cut everything in half lengthwise
3. Toss everything with olive oil and place onto a prepared baking sheet
4. Roast for 18-20 minutes at 400 F or until golden brown
5. When ready remove from the oven and serve

SOUP RECIPES

ZUCCHINI SOUP

Serves: **4**

Prep Time: **10** Minutes

Cook Time: **20** Minutes

Total Time: **30** Minutes

INGREDIENTS

- 1 tablespoon olive oil
- 1 lb. zucchini
- ¼ red onion
- ½ cup all-purpose flour
- ¼ tsp salt
- ¼ tsp pepper
- 1 can vegetable broth
- 1 cup heavy cream

DIRECTIONS

1. In a saucepan heat olive oil and sauté zucchini until tender
2. Add remaining ingredients to the saucepan and bring to a boil
3. When all the vegetables are tender transfer to a blender and blend until smooth
4. Pour soup into bowls, garnish with parsley and serve

Serves: **4**

Prep Time: **10** Minutes

Cook Time: **60** Minutes

Total Time: **70** Minutes

INGREDIENTS

- 1 head cauliflower
- 1 clove garlic
- 1 tsp sage
- ½ tsp black pepper
- 5 cups chicken stock
- 1 head garlic
- 1 tsp olive oil
- 1 cup onion
- 1 cup apple
- 1 tsp thyme
- 1 tsp rosemary
- 8 baguette slices

DIRECTIONS

1. Preheat oven to 325 F
2. Drizzle garlic head with olive oil and wrap in aluminum foil and roast for 25-30 minutes

3. Place baguette slices on a baking sheet and toast for 10-12 minutes
4. Squeeze the softened garlic cloves on the baguette slices
5. In a sauce pan add vegetables, spices, chicken stock and bring to boil
6. Reduce heat ad simmer for 20-30 minutes
7. With a blender, puree soup and garnish with garlic
8. Serve with baguette slices

CHICKEN STEW WITH MUSHROOMS

Serves: **4**

Prep Time: **10**   Minutes

Cook Time: **30**   Minutes

Total Time: **40**   Minutes

INGREDIENTS

- ½ cup onion
- 1 cup cooked chicken
- 1 cup no-salt chicken stock
- ¼ tablespoon seasoning
- ¼ tsp paprika
- ½ tsp garlic powder
- ¼ tsp black pepper
- 1 tablespoon cornstarch
- ¼ cup milk
- 1 clove garlic
- ¼ cup red pepper
- ¼ cup shitake mushrooms
- ¼ cup button mushrooms
- 1 cup kale
- 1 tablespoon olive oil

DIRECTIONS

1. Sauté the onions and garlic together in a skillet
2. Add onions and the rest of vegetables
3. Sauté until they are soft
4. Add chicken stock, spices, cooked chicken and dry spices
5. In another container mix milk and cornstarch
6. Add to stew and simmer
7. When ready serve with rice or noodles

CHILI THAI SAUCE

Serves: *4*

Prep Time: *10*   Minutes

Cook Time: *10*   Minutes

Total Time: *20*   Minutes

INGREDIENTS

- 1 cup water
- 1 tsp pepper flakes
- 1 tsp ketchup
- 3 tsp cornstarch
- ¾ cup vinegar
- ¼ cup sugar
- 1 tsp ginger
- 1 tsp garlic
- 1 tsp garlic

DIRECTIONS

1. Boil water and vinegar
2. Add ginger, garlic, sugar, red pepper flakes and ketchup
3. Simmer for 5-10 minutes, add cornstarch and continue stirring, remove and serve

Serves: *4*

Prep Time: *10*   Minutes

Cook Time: *20*   Minutes

Total Time: *30*   Minutes

INGREDIENTS

- 2 tablespoons olive oil
- 1 onion
- 1 baguette
- ½ bunch arugula
- 1 tablespoon wine vinegar
- 3 cloves garlic
- ½ tsp hot pepper flakes
- 1 lb. beef

DIRECTIONS

1. Mix vinegar, oil, garlic and pepper flakes in a bag and set aside
2. Add meat to marinade and refrigerate overnight
3. Remove steak from bag and grill steak for 4-5 minutes per side
4. Fry onion in a skillet and toss with marinade
5. Slice steak and top with onions and arugula

Serves: *2*

Prep Time: *10*   Minutes

Cook Time: *10*   Minutes

Total Time: *20*   Minutes

INGREDIENTS

- 3 Panini buns
- 1 cup egg plant
- 1 cup cooked roast beef
- 2 tablespoons mayonnaise
- 1 tablespoon pesto sauce

DIRECTIONS

1. Slice buns in half
2. In a bowl mix pesto sauce and mayonnaise and spread on each bun
3. Top with vegetables and roast beef

TOFU STIR-FRY

Serves: **4**

Prep Time: **10**   Minutes

Cook Time: **10**   Minutes

Total Time: **20**   Minutes

INGREDIENTS

- 1 cup white rice
- 1 tablespoon hoisin sauce
- 1 tablespoon rice vinegar
- 1 tsp cornstarch
- 1 cloves garlic
- 1 jalapeno pepper
- ½ cup basil leaves
- 3 tablespoons canola oil
- 1 package tofu
- 1 eggplant
- 3 scallions

DIRECTIONS

1. Cook rice following the package instructions
2. In a skillet heat 1 tablespoon oil, add tofu and cook for 10-12 minutes
3. Transfer to a plate

4. Add vegetables and cook until tender, add sauce, toss and toss until thickened
5. Serve with basil and rice

Serves: **2**

Prep Time: **10**   Minutes

Cook Time: **15**   Minutes

Total Time: **25**   Minutes

INGREDIENTS

- 12 asparagus
- 1 lemon juice
- 1 tablespoon sesame oil
- 1 tsp sesame seeds

DIRECTIONS

1. In a bowl mix lemon juice, sesame oil and sesame seeds
2. Wrap in tinfoil and bake at 350 for 15 minutes or until tender
3. Remove and serve

Serves:　　　**2**

Prep Time:　**10**　Minutes

Cook Time:　**20**　Minutes

Total Time:　**30**　Minutes

INGREDIENTS

- 1/3 lb. pasta
- ½ cup Parmesan cheese
- ½ cup olive oil
- 1 cup basil
- 2 cloves garlic
- ½ cup pine nuts

DIRECTIONS

1. Cook pasta and set aside
2. In a bowl mix garlic, pine nuts and basil
3. Mix with Parmesan cheese and add oil
4. Serve over pasta

COUSCOUS SALAD

Serves: *1*
Prep Time: *10* Minutes

Cook Time: *10* Minutes

Total Time: *20* Minutes

INGREDIENTS

- 3 cup water
- ¼ tsp cumin
- 1 tablespoon honey
- 1 tsp lemon juice
- 1 green onion
- 1 carrot
- ¼ red pepper
- cilantro
- ½ tsp cinnamon
- 2 cups couscous
- 1 tsp olive oil

DIRECTIONS

1. Bring water boil add cumin, honey, cinnamon, add couscous and lemon juice
2. Cover and remove from heat
3. Add hers, olive oil, vegetables and serve

TOFU STICKS

Serves: **4**

Prep Time: **10** Minutes

Cook Time: **25** Minutes

Total Time: **35** Minutes

INGREDIENTS

- 1 tsp tamari sauce
- 1 tsp seasoning
- 1 cup tofu
- 1 tablespoon water
- ¼ cup cornflake crumbs

DIRECTIONS

1. In a bowl mix tamari with water
2. In another bowl mix cornflake and seasoning
3. Dip tofu into tamari sauce and then into seasoning
4. Place tofu slices on a baking sheet and bake at 325 for 15-18 minutes, remove and serve

Serves: **4**

Prep Time: **10** Minutes

Cook Time: **25** Minutes

Total Time: **35** Minutes

INGREDIENTS
- 1 eggplant
- 1 cup cornmeal
- ¼ tsp oregano
- ¼ tsp garlic powder
- ¼ tsp paprika
- 1 tsp olive oil
- 1 egg

DIRECTIONS

1. Preheat oven to 375 F
2. In a bowl mix garlic powder, cornmeal, oregano and paprika
3. In a bowl beat the egg
4. Dip the eggplant fries in the beaten eggs and transfer to the cornmeal mixture
5. Place the eggplant fried on a baking sheet and bake for 20 minutes, remove and serve

Serves: **4**

Prep Time: **10**   Minutes

Cook Time: **10**   Minutes

Total Time: **20**   Minutes

INGREDIENTS

- 2 pita rounds
- 2 tablespoons olive oil
- chili powder

DIRECTIONS

1. Cut each pita into 8 wedges
2. Brush with olive oil and sprinkle with chili powder
3. Bake at 325 F for 12 minutes or until crisp
4. Remove and serve

Serves: **2**

Prep Time: **10** Minutes

Cook Time: **10** Minutes

Total Time: **20** Minutes

INGREDIENTS

- 1 cup roasted red peppers
- 1 tablespoon olive oil
- 1 tsp lemon juice
- 1 clove garlic
- 1 tsp cumin

DIRECTIONS

1. In a blender mix all ingredients and blend until smooth
2. Remove and serve with pita chips

Serves: 2
Prep Time: 5   Minutes

Cook Time: 15   Minutes

Total Time: 20   Minutes

INGREDIENTS

- 4 oz. spaghetti
- 2 cups basil leaves
- 2 garlic cloves
- ¼ cup olive oil
- 2 tablespoons parmesan cheese
- ½ tsp black pepper

DIRECTIONS

1. Bring water to a boil and add pasta
2. In a blend add parmesan cheese, basil leaves, garlic and blend
3. Add olive oil, pepper and blend again
4. Pour pesto onto pasta and serve when ready

Serves: *4*

Prep Time: *10*   Minutes

Cook Time: *30*   Minutes

Total Time: *40*   Minutes

INGREDIENTS

- 4 fennel bulbs
- 1 tablespoon olive oil
- 1 tsp salt

DIRECTIONS

1. Slice the fennel bulb lengthwise into thick slices
2. Drizzle with olive oil and salt
3. Place the fennel bulb into a baking dish
4. Bake at 375 F for 25-30 minutes
5. When ready remove from the oven and serve

SPICED CAULIFLOWER

Serves: **4**

Prep Time: **10**   Minutes

Cook Time: **30**   Minutes

Total Time: **40**   Minutes

INGREDIENTS

- 1 head cauliflower
- 2 tablespoons olive oil
- 1 tsp smoked paprika
- ¼ tsp cumin
- ¼ tsp coriander
- ¼ tsp salt
- ¼ tsp black pepper

DIRECTIONS

1. In a bowl toss the cauliflower with olive oil, paprika, cumin, coriander, salt and pepper
2. Spread the cauliflower on a baking sheet
3. Bake for 20 minutes at 400 F
4. When ready remove from the oven and serve

ROASTED BUTTERNUT SQUASH

Serves: *1*

Prep Time: *10*   Minutes

Cook Time: *35*   Minutes

Total Time: *45*   Minutes

INGREDIENTS

- 1 butternut squash
- 2 shallots
- 2 tablespoons olive oil
- 1 tsp rosemary
- ½ tsp salt
- ¼ tsp black pepper

DIRECTIONS

1. In a bowl combine all ingredients together
2. Add the butternut squash in the mixture and let it marinate for 10-15 minutes
3. Bake for 20 minutes at 425 F
4. When ready remove from the oven and serve

FRIED CHICKEN

Serves: **4**

Prep Time: **10**   Minutes

Cook Time: **20**   Minutes

Total Time: **30**   Minutes

INGREDIENTS

- 2 chicken breasts
- ½ cup almond flour
- 1 tsp salt
- 1 tsp black pepper
- 2 eggs
- 1 cup bread crumbs
- ½ cup parmesan cheese

DIRECTIONS

1. In a bowl combine flour, salt and pepper
2. In another bowl beat eggs and add to the flour mixture
3. Cut chicken breasts into thin slices and dip into the flour mixture
4. In another bowl combine bread crumbs and parmesan cheese
5. Take the chicken slices and dip into bread crumbs mixture
6. Place the chicken in frying pan and cook until golden brown
7. When ready remove from the pan and serve

Serves: **4-6**

Prep Time: **10** Minutes

Cook Time: **40** Minutes

Total Time: **50** Minutes

INGREDIENTS

- 1 whole chicken
- 1 celery
- 1 onion
- 4 cloves garlic
- 1 sprig of rosemary
- 1 bay leaf
- 1 tablespoon olive oil
- 1 tsp salt
- 1 tsp black pepper

DIRECTIONS

1. In a pot heat olive oil and sauté onion, garlic and celery
2. Add chicken, rosemary, bay leaf, salt, black pepper and cook for 4-5 minutes
3. Remove from the pot and transfer to the oven
4. Bake for 30-35 minutes at 325 F
5. When ready remove from the oven and serve

GLAZED SALMON

Serves: *1*

Prep Time: *10*   Minutes

Cook Time: *30*   Minutes

Total Time: *40*   Minutes

INGREDIENTS

- 1 salmon
- ¼ cup brown sugar
- 1 tablespoon lemon zest
- 1 tsp salt
- 1 tsp black pepper

DIRECTIONS

1. In a bowl combine sugar, lemon zest, salt and pepper
2. Spread the mixture over the salmon and rub with the mixture
3. Bake at 350 F for 20-25 minutes
4. When ready remove from the oven and serve

FISH TACOS

Serves: **8-12**

Prep Time: **10** Minutes

Cook Time: **30** Minutes

Total Time: **40** Minutes

INGREDIENTS

- 1 cup bread crumbs
- ¼ cup parmesan cheese
- 1 cup almond flour
- 2 eggs
- 2 tablespoons almond milk
- 1 lb. cod fish
- Tortillas
- 1 tsp Salt

DIRECTIONS

1. In a bowl combine pepper, salt and flour
2. In another bowl whisk to eggs with milk
3. In another bowl combine bread crumbs with parmesan cheese
4. Cut the fish into thin strips and dip first into the flour mixture bowl, then egg mixture bowl and then into the bread crumbs mixture bowl
5. Fry for 5-6 minutes each fish strip or until golden brown

6. When ready transfer to a plate and serve

SIMPLE STEAK

Serves: **4-6**

Prep Time: **10**   Minutes

Cook Time: **20**   Minutes

Total Time: **30**   Minutes

INGREDIENTS

- 1 can celery soup
- 1 lb. cube steaks
- ¼ cup red onion
- 4 garlic cloves
- 1 stalk celery
- ¼ cup carrot
- 1 tsp cumin
- 1 tsp coriander
- salt

DIRECTIONS

1. In a pan heat olive oil and sauté onion, cloves, celery and carrot
2. In a bowl combine celery soup with sautéed vegetables
3. Brown the cube steaks and set aside
4. Pour the sautéed vegetables and mixture into a pan, add cube steaks and cook until vegetables are soft
5. When ready remove from heat and serve

CHEESE PESTO

Serves: **2**

Prep Time: **5**   Minutes

Cook Time: **5**   Minutes

Total Time: **10**   Minutes

INGREDIENTS

- 1 can spinach
- ¼ cup water
- ¼ cup cottage cheese
- ¼ cup basil
- 2 tablespoon parmesan cheese
- 1 tablespoon olive oil
- 3 cloves garlic
- 1 tsp black pepper

DIRECTIONS

1. Place all ingredients in a blender and blend until smooth
2. When ready serve with cooked pasta

Serves: **1**

Prep Time: **5** Minutes

Cook Time: **5** Minutes

Total Time: **10** Minutes

INGREDIENTS

- 2 cups arugula leaves
- ¼ cup cranberries
- ¼ cup honey
- ¼ cup pecans
- 1 cup salad dressing

DIRECTIONS

1. In a bowl combine all ingredients together and mix well
2. Serve with dressing

Serves: *1*
Prep Time: 5   Minutes

Cook Time: 5   Minutes

Total Time: *10* Minutes

INGREDIENTS

- ¼ cup masoor
- ¼ cup cucumber
- ½ cup carrot
- ¼ cup tomatoes
- ¼ cup onion

SALAD DRESSING

- ¼ tablespoon olive oil
- 1 tsp lemon juice
- ¼ tsp green chillies

DIRECTIONS

1. In a bowl combine all ingredients together and mix well
2. Add salad dressing, toss well and serve

Serves: **4**

Prep Time: **10**   Minutes

Cook Time: **5**   Minutes

Total Time: **15**   Minutes

INGREDIENTS

Salad

- 3 tbs basil leaves
- 100g Kalamata olives
- 3 tbs pine nuts
- 2 green shallots
- ½ sun dried tomato
- 1 cup rice

Dressing

- 3 tbs oil
- Pepper
- 2 tbs mustard
- 3 tbs lemon juice
- Salt
- 1 clove garlic

DIRECTIONS

1. **Cook the rice**

2. Mix the dressing ingredients together
3. Mix the salad ingredients with the rice in a bowl
4. Add the dressing and serve

TUNA SALAD

Serves: **4**

Prep Time: **10** Minutes

Cook Time: **30** Minutes

Total Time: **40** Minutes

INGREDIENTS

- 2 5OZ. can tuna
- 1/3 cup mayonnaise
- ¼ cup chopped Kalamata
- 2 tablespoons red onion
- 2 tablespoons red peppers
- 2 tablespoons basil
- 1 tablespoon capers
- 1 tablespoon lemon juice

DIRECTIONS

1. In a bowl combine all ingredients together and mix well
2. Serve when ready

SALMON SALAD

Serves: **2**

Prep Time: **10**   Minutes

Cook Time: **10**   Minutes

Total Time: **20**   Minutes

INGREDIENTS

- 2 salmon fillets
- 1 cup cucumber
- 1 red onion
- 1 tablespoon capers
- 1 tablespoon dill
- 1 tablespoon balsamic vinegar
- 1 tablespoon olive oil
- ¼ tsp pepper

DIRECTIONS

1. In a bowl add salmon, cucumber, capers, red onion and toss
2. In a jar add olive oil, vinegar and pour over salmon, toss again

Serves: **4**

Prep Time: **10** Minutes

Cook Time: **50** Minutes

Total Time: **60** Minutes

INGREDIENTS

- 1 pint fresh strawberries
- 1 red apple
- 1 sweet potato
- 1 large onion
- 1 tablespoon coconut oil
- 1 chopped cabbage
- ½ cup tomatoes
- 1 tablespoon almonds
- 1 tablespoon basil
- 2 tsp orange zest
- 1 banana

DIRECTIONS

1. Preheat the oven to 375 F and place the strawberries on a baking sheet
2. On another baking sheet place, the potatoes and onions

3. Rub all the ingredients with with coconut oil and place them in the oven for 45-50 minutes

4. Remove from the oven and scoop out the sweet potato flesh

5. In a bowl mix tomato, almonds, cabbage, apple and basil

6. In a blender puree the roasted strawberries and banana pour over the salad mixture and toss to combine

Serves: **2**

Prep Time: **10**   Minutes

Cook Time: **10**   Minutes

Total Time: **20**   Minutes

INGREDIENTS

- 1 head cauliflower
- 1 tablespoon avocado oil
- 3 cups salad greens
- 1/3 cup red onion
- 1 pear
- harissa sauce
- 1 green bell
- 1 tablespoon parsley
- 1 tablespoon lemon zest
- 1 head Swiss chard
- 1 tomato

DIRECTIONS

1. Preheat oven to 375 F and place the cauliflower on a baking sheet and drizzle with oil and salt
2. Roast for 35-40 minutes and remove when ready

3. In a bowl mix pepper, onion, parsley, Swiss chard, tomato and the roasted cauliflower

4. In another bowl whisk the lemon juice with harissa sauce and drizzle the dressing over salad

Serves: **2**

Prep Time: **10**   Minutes

Cook Time: **10**   Minutes

Total Time: **20**   Minutes

INGREDIENTS

- 2 lbs. green beans
- juice of 1 orange
- 1 tsp orange zest
- 2 carrots
- 1 apple
- 2 stalks celery

DIRECTIONS

1. Stem the beans in pot over medium heat for 5-6 minutes and remove when ready
2. Add the carrots to the bowl and the steamed greens beans, celery and apple
3. In another bowl mix pepper, salt, orange juice and drizzle over the salad mixture

FISH STEW

Serves: **4**

Prep Time: **15** Minutes

Cook Time: **45** Minutes

Total Time: **60** Minutes

INGREDIENTS

- 1 fennel bulb
- 1 red onion
- 2 garlic cloves
- 2 tablespoons olive oil
- 1 cup white wine
- 1 tablespoon fennel seeds
- 4 bay leaves
- 2 cups chicken stock
- 8 oz. halibut
- 12 oz. haddock

DIRECTIONS

1. Chop all ingredients in big chunks

2. In a large pot heat olive oil and add ingredients one by one
3. Cook for 5-6 or until slightly brown
4. Add remaining ingredients and cook until tender, 35-45 minutes
5. Season while stirring on low heat
6. When ready remove from heat and serve

BUTTERNUT SQUASH STEW

Serves: **4**

Prep Time: **15**   Minutes

Cook Time: **45**   Minutes

Total Time: **60**   Minutes

INGREDIENTS

- 2 tablespoons olive oil
- 2 red onions
- 2 cloves garlic
- 1. Tablespoon rosemary
- 1 tablespoon thyme
- 2 lb. beef
- 1 cup white wine
- 1 cup butternut squash
- 2 cups beef broth
- ½ cup tomatoes

DIRECTIONS

1. Chop all ingredients in big chunks
2. In a large pot heat olive oil and add ingredients one by one
3. Cook for 5-6 or until slightly brown
4. Add remaining ingredients and cook until tender, 35-45 minutes

5. Season while stirring on low heat
6. When ready remove from heat and serve

CASSEROLE RECIPES

BACON CASSEROLE

Serves: **4**

Prep Time: **10**   Minutes

Cook Time: **15**   Minutes

Total Time: **25**   Minutes

INGREDIENTS

- 4-5 slices bacon
- 3-4 tablespoons butter
- 5-6 tablespoons flour
- 2 cups milk
- 3 cups cheddar cheese
- 2 cups chicken breast
- 1 tsp seasoning mix

DIRECTIONS

1. Sauté the veggies and set aside
2. Preheat the oven to 425 F
3. Transfer the sautéed veggies to a baking dish, add remaining ingredients to the baking dish
4. Mix well, add seasoning and place the dish in the oven
5. Bake for 12-15 minutes or until slightly brown

6. When ready remove from the oven and serve

CHICKEN CASSEROLE

Serves: **4**

Prep Time: **10**   Minutes

Cook Time: **40**   Minutes

Total Time: **50**   Minutes

INGREDIENTS

- 1 cup Greek yogurt
- ½ cup grape juice
- 1 cup mushroom soup
- 1 cup cooked rice

DIRECTIONS

1. In a bowl add mushrooms, yogurt, grape juice and combine
2. Place the chicken breast in a prepare baking dish and pour the mixture over the chicken
3. Bake for 35-40 minutes at 325 F
4. When ready remove from the oven and serve with rice

ENCHILADA CASSEROLE

Serves: **4**

Prep Time: **10**   Minutes

Cook Time: **25**   Minutes

Total Time: **35**   Minutes

INGREDIENTS

- 1 tablespoon olive oil
- 1 red onion
- 1 bell pepper
- 2 cloves garlic
- 1 can black beans
- 1 cup chicken
- 1 can green chilis
- 1 can enchilada sauce
- 1 cup cheddar cheese
- 1 cup sour cream

DIRECTIONS

1. Sauté the veggies and set aside
2. Preheat the oven to 425 F
3. Transfer the sautéed veggies to a baking dish, add remaining ingredients to the baking dish
4. Mix well, add seasoning and place the dish in the oven

5. Bake for 15-25 minutes or until slightly brown
6. When ready remove from the oven and serve

CASSEROLE PIZZA

Serves: **6-8**

Prep Time: **10** Minutes

Cook Time: **15** Minutes

Total Time: **25** Minutes

INGREDIENTS

- 1 pizza crust
- ½ cup tomato sauce
- ¼ black pepper
- 1 cup zucchini slices
- 1 cup mozzarella cheese
- 1 cup olives

DIRECTIONS

1. Spread tomato sauce on the pizza crust
2. Place all the toppings on the pizza crust
3. Bake the pizza at 425 F for 12-15 minutes
4. When ready remove pizza from the oven and serve

SECOND COOKBOOK

PUMPKIN CUPCAKES

Serves: **4**

Prep Time: **10**   Minutes

Cook Time: **30**   Minutes

Total Time: **40**   Minutes

INGREDIENTS

- 1 cup pumpkin puree
- 1 tsp cinnamon
- ½ tsp mixed spice
- 1 tsp ginger
- ¼ lb. butter
- 1 cups brown sugar
- 2 eggs
- 2 cups flour
- 3 tsp baking powder

DIRECTIONS

1. Boil the pumpkin and then puree in a food processor

2. Cream butter and sugar, add the eggs and beat well, stir in pureed pumpkin and dry ingredients
3. Combine all ingredients and spoon mixture into a muffin tin
4. Bake at 300 F for 20 minutes, remove and serve

BUCKWHEAT PANCAKES

Serves: *2*

Prep Time: *10*   Minutes

Cook Time: *10*   Minutes

Total Time: *20*   Minutes

INGREDIENTS

- 1 cup buckwheat mix
- 1 egg
- 1 cup milk
- 1 tablespoon butter

DIRECTIONS

1. In a bow mix all ingredients, add olive oil and pour batter
2. Cook for 1-2 minutes per side
3. Remove and serve

Serves: **4**

Prep Time: **10**   Minutes

Cook Time: **40**   Minutes

Total Time: **50**   Minutes

INGREDIENTS

- 1 cup whole meal self raising flour
- 1 cup brown sugar
- 1 cup self raising flour
- 1 tsp salt
- 1 tsp cinnamon
- 1 tsp ginger
- 1 cup olive oil
- 2 cups carrots
- 3 eggs
- ½ tsp allspice

DIRECTIONS

1. Preheat oven to 275 F and place all ingredients in a bowl except eggs
2. In another bowl mix eggs and add to the mixture
3. Pour into cake in
4. For carrot cake pour batter into cupcake molds

5. Bake for 40 minutes
6. Remove and serve

RUSSIAN FUDGE

Serves: **2**

Prep Time: **10** Minutes

Cook Time: **30** Minutes

Total Time: **40** Minutes

INGREDIENTS

- ½ butter
- 1 can condensed milk
- ¾ cup milk
- 2 tablespoons golden syrup
- 3 cups sugar
- 1 tablespoon vanilla essence

DIRECTIONS

1. In a pot place all the ingredients except vanilla essence and bring to boil
2. Boil for 15-20 minutes and in another bowl drop some fudge mixture
3. Add vanilla essence and beat with a mixer for 5-6 minutes
4. Pour into greased tin and place in fridge
5. Cut into pieces and serve

Serves: **2**
Prep Time: **10**   Minutes

Cook Time: **20**   Minutes

Total Time: **30**   Minutes

INGREDIENTS

- 1-inch ginger
- 4 tablespoons brown sugar
- 1 tsp citric acid
- 1 L soda water
- fresh mint

DIRECTIONS

1. Grate ginger and mix with the rest of ingredients and let them sit for 10-12 minutes
2. Serve when ready

Serves: **4**

Prep Time: **10**   Minutes

Cook Time: **30**   Minutes

Total Time: **40**   Minutes

INGREDIENTS

- 2 cups self raising flour
- 2 tablespoons butter
- 2/3 cups milk

FILLING

- 1/3 cup butter
- ¾ cup brown sugar
- 1 tsp cinnamon

DIRECTIONS

1. Preheat oven to 350 F
2. In a blender add butter, flour and blend until smooth
3. Add milk and blend or another 1-2 minutes
4. Remove mixture onto floured surface
5. In the blender put all ingredients for the filling and blend until smooth
6. Spread the filling into the dough

Serves: **4**

Prep Time: **10** Minutes

Cook Time: **30** Minutes

Total Time: **40** Minutes

INGREDIENTS

- 1 leek
- 1 clove garlic
- sat
- citric acid
- 1 tsp turmeric
- 1 tsp cumin
- 1 tsp coriander powder
- ½ cup roasted sunflower seeds
- 1 tablespoon rice flour
- 1 tsp arrowroot
- 1 cup broccoli
- 2 tablespoons butter
- 1 cup milk
- macaroni pasta

DIRECTIONS

1. Cook pasta, add leek and sauté with butter, citric acid and pepper
2. Add butter, cumin, coriander powder, turmeric, sunflower seeds
3. Add arrowroot and rice flour and cook for 2-3 minutes
4. Add broccoli, pasta and stir
5. Cook for 20 minutes at 350 F, remove and serve

Serves: **4**

Prep Time: **10**   Minutes

Cook Time: **20**   Minutes

Total Time: **30**   Minutes

INGREDIENTS

- rice noodles
- onion
- cucumber
- carrot
- Coriander
- zucchini
- carrot
- Thai mint
- Chives
- Roasted sunflower seeds
- ginger
- rice paper
- tofu

DIRECTIONS

1. **In a bowl place the noodles and boil, cover with a lid**

2. When they are cool set aside, soak a couple of rice papers in warm water and place the rice paper on a towel

3. Place the noodles and the rest of rest of ingredients on a rice paper and fold

4. Serve when ready

Serves: **4**

Prep Time: **10** Minutes

Cook Time: **30** Minutes

Total Time: **40** Minutes

INGREDIENTS

- ¼ lb. butter
- ½ cup sugar
- 1 cup plain flour
- ½ whole meal flour
- 1 tsp baking powder
- 1 tsp ginger

DIRECTIONS

1. In a food processor add butter and soon and blend until smooth
2. Add the rest of ingredients and blend
3. Remove from blender and bake for 20 minutes at 350 F
4. Cut into cookie shape and serve

CORNMEAL WAFFELS

Serves: **2**

Prep Time: **10** Minutes

Cook Time: **10** Minutes

Total Time: **20** Minutes

INGREDIENTS

- 1 cup corn flour
- 1 egg
- 1 cup milk
- 1 tablespoon butter
- 2 tablespoons honey
- ½ cup rice flour
- 1 tsp baking powder
- ½ tsp salt

DIRECTIONS

1. Let sit for 8-10 minutes
2. Place in the waffle iron and cook
3. Remove and serve

CHEESE CAKE

Serves: **4**

Prep Time: **10**   Minutes

Cook Time: **30**   Minutes

Total Time: **40**   Minutes

INGREDIENTS

- ½ lb. gingernut biscuits
- ½ lb. blueberries
- 1 tsp vanilla extract
- 1 tsp acid
- ¼ lb. butter
- ¼ lb. caster sugar
- 2 tablespoons arrowroot
- ¼ lb. full-fat Philadelphia
- 2 eggs

DIRECTIONS

1. Preheat oven to 350 F
2. In a bowl mix butter and biscuits and press into the base of the tin
3. Bake for 10-12 minutes
4. In a saucepan cook blueberry with sugar and milk for 10-12 minutes

5. Take off heat add citric acid and vanilla
6. Bake for 40 minutes remove and let it chill

BASIC WAFFLES

Serves: **2**

Prep Time: **10**   Minutes

Cook Time: **10**   Minutes

Total Time: **20**   Minutes

INGREDIENTS

- 2 eggs
- 1 tablespoon sugar
- 1 tablespoon baking powder
- 1 cup flour
- 1/8 cup milk
- ½ tsp vanilla essence

DIRECTIONS

1. In a food processor add all the ingredients and blend until smooth
2. Heat the waffle iron pour in the batter
3. Cook until golden
4. Serve with maple syrup

CARAMEL POPCORN

Serves: **4**

Prep Time: **10** Minutes

Cook Time: **20** Minutes

Total Time: **30** Minutes

INGREDIENTS

- 1 tablespoon olive oil
- 4 tablespoons popcorn kernels

CARAMEL SAUCE

- 1 tablespoon butter
- 1 tablespoon brown sugar
- 1 tablespoon golden syrup

DIRECTIONS

1. In a saucepan pour olive oil and popcorn kernels over medium heat and cover
2. Shake the saucepan to distribute evenly
3. In another saucepan melt the caramel sauce ingredients
4. Remove from heat and pour over your popcorn

Serves: **4**

Prep Time: **10** Minutes

Cook Time: **10** Minutes

Total Time: **20** Minutes

INGREDIENTS

- ½ tsp salt
- 1 cup plain flour
- 1 tsp olive oil
- 1 onion
- ½ cup hot water
- 1 tablespoon cold water

DIRECTIONS

1. In a bowl mix all ingredients
2. Pour mixture into a pan and cook for 1-2 minutes per side
3. Remove and serve

TOASTED MUESLI

Serves: **4**

Prep Time: **10**   Minutes

Cook Time: **60**   Minutes

Total Time: **70**   Minutes

INGREDIENTS

- 2 cups oats
- 1 cup oat mix
- ½ cup sunflower seeds
- ½ cup sunflower oil

DIRECTIONS

1. In a bowl mix all ingredients
2. Bake for 60 minutes at 275 F
3. Garnish with blueberries and serve

GINGERBREAD BISCUITS

Serves: **4**
Prep Time: **10** Minutes

Cook Time: **30** Minutes

Total Time: **40** Minutes

INGREDIENTS

- 2 oz. butter
- 1 cup self raising flour
- ½ tsp salt
- 3 tablespoons ginger
- ½ cup milk
- 1 egg beaten
- 1 tablespoon vanilla extract
- ½ cup golden syrup
- ½ cup maple syrup
- ½ cup honey

DIRECTIONS

1. Preheat oven to 300 F
2. In a pan melt honey, butter, syrup and set aside
3. White syrup mixture is cooling, grate the ginger and add to the syrup mixture
4. Add flour, salt, milk, egg and vanilla extract

5. Form small cookies and bake for 15-18 minutes at 300 F
6. Remove and serve

VANILLA CHIA PUDDING

Serves: **4**

Prep Time: **10** Minutes

Cook Time: **10** Minutes

Total Time: **20** Minutes

INGREDIENTS

- 2 cups hemp milk
- 2 packets stevia
- ½ tsp cinnamon
- ½ cup chia seeds
- 1 tablespoon vanilla extract

DIRECTIONS

1. In a bowl whisk all ingredients together
2. Let it chill overnight and serve

APPLE PANCAKES

Serves: **4**

Prep Time: **10** Minutes

Cook Time: **20** Minutes

Total Time: **30** Minutes

INGREDIENTS

- 1 cup whole wheat flour
- ¼ tsp baking soda
- ¼ tsp baking powder
- 1 cup apples
- 2 eggs
- 1 cup milk

DIRECTIONS

1. In a bowl combine all ingredients together and mix well
2. In a skillet heat olive oil
3. Pour ¼ of the batter and cook each pancake for 1-2 minutes per side
4. When ready remove from heat and serve

APRICOTS PANCAKES

Serves: **4**

Prep Time: **10** Minutes

Cook Time: **30** Minutes

Total Time: **40** Minutes

INGREDIENTS

- 1 cup whole wheat flour
- ¼ tsp baking soda
- ¼ tsp baking powder
- 1 cup apricots
- 2 eggs
- 1 cup milk

DIRECTIONS

1. In a bowl combine all ingredients together and mix well
2. In a skillet heat olive oil
3. Pour ¼ of the batter and cook each pancake for 1-2 minutes per side
4. When ready remove from heat and serve

ACEROLA PANCAKES

Serves: **4**

Prep Time: **10**   Minutes

Cook Time: **20**   Minutes

Total Time: **30**   Minutes

INGREDIENTS

- 1 cup whole wheat flour
- ¼ tsp baking soda
- ¼ tsp baking powder
- 1 cup acerola
- 2 eggs
- 1 cup milk

DIRECTIONS

1. In a bowl combine all ingredients together and mix well
2. In a skillet heat olive oil
3. Pour ¼ of the batter and cook each pancake for 1-2 minutes per side
4. When ready remove from heat and serve

Serves: **8-12**

Prep Time: **10**   Minutes

Cook Time: **20**   Minutes

Total Time: **30**   Minutes

INGREDIENTS

- 2 eggs
- 1 tablespoon olive oil
- 1 cup milk
- 2 cups whole wheat flour
- 1 tsp baking soda
- ¼ tsp baking soda
- 1 tsp cinnamon
- 1 cup java-plum

DIRECTIONS

1. In a bowl combine all dry ingredients
2. In another bowl combine all dry ingredients
3. Combine wet and dry ingredients together
4. Pour mixture into 8-12 prepared muffin cups, fill 2/3 of the cups
5. Bake for 18-20 minutes at 375 F
6. When ready remove from the oven and serve

KIWI MUFFINS

Serves: **8-12**

Prep Time: **10** Minutes

Cook Time: **20** Minutes

Total Time: **30** Minutes

INGREDIENTS

- 2 eggs
- 1 tablespoon olive oil
- 1 cup milk
- 2 cups whole wheat flour
- 1 tsp baking soda
- ¼ tsp baking soda
- 1 tsp cinnamon
- 1 cup kiwi

DIRECTIONS

1. In a bowl combine all dry ingredients
2. In another bowl combine all dry ingredients
3. Combine wet and dry ingredients together
4. Pour mixture into 8-12 prepared muffin cups, fill 2/3 of the cups
5. Bake for 18-20 minutes at 375 F
6. When ready remove from the oven and serve

CHOCOLATE MUFFINS

Serves: **8-12**

Prep Time: **10**   Minutes

Cook Time: **20**   Minutes

Total Time: **30**   Minutes

INGREDIENTS

- 2 eggs
- 1 tablespoon olive oil
- 1 cup milk
- 2 cups whole wheat flour
- 1 tsp baking soda
- ¼ tsp baking soda
- 1 tsp cinnamon
- 1 cup chocolate chips

DIRECTIONS

1. In a bowl combine all dry ingredients
2. In another bowl combine all dry ingredients
3. Combine wet and dry ingredients together
4. Pour mixture into 8-12 prepared muffin cups, fill 2/3 of the cups
5. Bake for 18-20 minutes at 375 F
6. When ready remove from the oven and serve

MANGO MUFFINS

Serves: **8-12**
Prep Time: **10**   Minutes

Cook Time: **20**   Minutes

Total Time: **30**   Minutes

INGREDIENTS

- 2 eggs
- 1 tablespoon olive oil
- 1 cup milk
- 2 cups whole wheat flour
- 1 tsp baking soda
- ¼ tsp baking soda
- 1 tsp cinnamon
- 1 cup mango

DIRECTIONS

1. In a bowl combine all dry ingredients
2. In another bowl combine all dry ingredients
3. Combine wet and dry ingredients together
4. Pour mixture into 8-12 prepared muffin cups, fill 2/3 of the cups
5. Bake for 18-20 minutes at 375 F
6. When ready remove from the oven and serve

BOK CHOY OMELETTE

Serves: *1*
Prep Time: *5*   Minutes
Cook Time: *10*   Minutes
Total Time: *15*   Minutes

INGREDIENTS

- 2 eggs
- ¼ tsp salt
- ¼ tsp black pepper
- 1 tablespoon olive oil
- ¼ cup cheese
- ¼ tsp basil
- 1 cup bok choy

DIRECTIONS

1. In a bowl combine all ingredients together and mix well
2. In a skillet heat olive oil and pour the egg mixture
3. Cook for 1-2 minutes per side
4. When ready remove omelette from the skillet and serve

BRUSSEL SPROUTS OMELETTE

Serves: *1*
Prep Time: *5*   Minutes

Cook Time: *10*   Minutes

Total Time: *15*   Minutes

INGREDIENTS

- 2 eggs
- ¼ tsp salt
- ¼ tsp black pepper
- 1 tablespoon olive oil
- ¼ cup cheese
- ¼ tsp basil
- 1 cup Brussel sprouts

DIRECTIONS

1. In a bowl combine all ingredients together and mix well
2. In a skillet heat olive oil and pour the egg mixture
3. Cook for 1-2 minutes per side
4. When ready remove omelette from the skillet and serve

CARROT OMELETTE

Serves: **1**

Prep Time: **5** Minutes

Cook Time: **10** Minutes

Total Time: **15** Minutes

INGREDIENTS

- 2 eggs
- ¼ tsp salt
- ¼ tsp black pepper
- 1 tablespoon olive oil
- ¼ cup cheese
- ¼ tsp basil
- 1 cup carrot

DIRECTIONS

1. In a bowl combine all ingredients together and mix well
2. In a skillet heat olive oil and pour the egg mixture
3. Cook for 1-2 minutes per side
4. When ready remove omelette from the skillet and serve

CORN OMELETTE

Serves: *1*

Prep Time: *5*   Minutes

Cook Time: *10*   Minutes

Total Time: *15*   Minutes

INGREDIENTS

- 2 eggs
- ¼ tsp salt
- ¼ tsp black pepper
- 1 tablespoon olive oil
- ¼ cup cheese
- ¼ tsp basil
- 1 cup corn

DIRECTIONS

1. In a bowl combine all ingredients together and mix well
2. In a skillet heat olive oil and pour the egg mixture
3. Cook for 1-2 minutes per side
4. When ready remove omelette from the skillet and serve

EGGPLANT OMELETTE

Serves: *1*
Prep Time: *5*   Minutes

Cook Time: *10*   Minutes

Total Time: *15*   Minutes

INGREDIENTS

- 2 eggs
- ¼ tsp salt
- ¼ tsp black pepper
- 1 tablespoon olive oil
- ¼ cup cheese
- ¼ tsp basil
- 1 cup eggplant

DIRECTIONS

1. In a bowl combine all ingredients together and mix well
2. In a skillet heat olive oil and pour the egg mixture
3. Cook for 1-2 minutes per side
4. When ready remove omelette from the skillet and serve

TART RECIPES

APPLE TART

Serves: **6-8**

Prep Time: **25** Minutes

Cook Time: **25** Minutes

Total Time: **50** Minutes

INGREDIENTS

- pastry sheets

FILLING

- 1 tsp lemon juice
- 3 oz. brown sugar
- 1 lb. apples
- 150 ml double cream
- 2 eggs

DIRECTIONS

5. Preheat oven to 400 F, unfold pastry sheets and place them on a baking sheet
6. Toss together all ingredients together and mix well
7. Spread mixture in a single layer on the pastry sheets
8. Before baking decorate with your desired fruits
9. Bake at 400 F for 22-25 minutes or until golden brown

10. When ready remove from the oven and serve

CHOCHOLATE TART

Serves: **6-8**

Prep Time: **25** Minutes

Cook Time: **25** Minutes

Total Time: **50** Minutes

INGREDIENTS

- pastry sheets
- 1 tsp vanilla extract
- ½ lb. caramel
- ½ lb. black chocolate
- 4-5 tablespoons butter
- 3 eggs
- ¼ lb. brown sugar

DIRECTIONS

11. Preheat oven to 400 F, unfold pastry sheets and place them on a baking sheet
12. Toss together all ingredients together and mix well
13. Spread mixture in a single layer on the pastry sheets
14. Before baking decorate with your desired fruits
15. Bake at 400 F for 22-25 minutes or until golden brown
16. When ready remove from the oven and serve

PEACH PECAN PIE

Serves: **8-12**

Prep Time: **15** Minutes

Cook Time: **35** Minutes

Total Time: **50** Minutes

INGREDIENTS

- 4-5 cups peaches
- 1 tablespoon preserves
- 1 cup sugar
- 4 small egg yolks
- ¼ cup flour
- 1 tsp vanilla extract

DIRECTIONS

1. Line a pie plate or pie form with pastry and cover the edges of the plate depending on your preference
2. In a bowl combine all pie ingredients together and mix well
3. Pour the mixture over the pastry
4. Bake at 400-425 F for 25-30 minutes or until golden brown
5. When ready remove from the oven and let it rest for 15 minutes

OREO PIE

Serves: **8-12**

Prep Time: **15** Minutes

Cook Time: **35** Minutes

Total Time: **50** Minutes

INGREDIENTS

- pastry sheets
- 6-8 oz. chocolate crumb piecrust
- 1 cup half-and-half
- 1 package instant pudding mix
- 10-12 Oreo cookies
- 10 oz. whipped topping

DIRECTIONS

1. Line a pie plate or pie form with pastry and cover the edges of the plate depending on your preference
2. In a bowl combine all pie ingredients together and mix well
3. Pour the mixture over the pastry
4. Bake at 400-425 F for 25-30 minutes or until golden brown
5. When ready remove from the oven and let it rest for 15 minutes

GRAPEFRUIT PIE

Serves: *8-12*

Prep Time: *15*   Minutes

Cook Time: *35*   Minutes

Total Time: *50*   Minutes

INGREDIENTS

- pastry sheets
- 2 cups grapefruit
- 1 cup brown sugar
- ¼ cup flour
- 5-6 egg yolks
- 5 oz. butter

DIRECTIONS

1. Line a pie plate or pie form with pastry and cover the edges of the plate depending on your preference
2. In a bowl combine all pie ingredients together and mix well
3. Pour the mixture over the pastry
4. Bake at 400-425 F for 25-30 minutes or until golden brown
5. When ready remove from the oven and let it rest for 15 minutes

BUTTERFINGER PIE

Serves: **8-12**

Prep Time: **15**   Minutes

Cook Time: **35**   Minutes

Total Time: **50**   Minutes

INGREDIENTS

- pastry sheets
- 1 package cream cheese
- 1 tsp vanilla extract
- ¼ cup peanut butter
- 1 cup powdered sugar (to decorate)
- 2 cups Butterfinger candy bars
- 8 oz whipped topping

DIRECTIONS

1. Line a pie plate or pie form with pastry and cover the edges of the plate depending on your preference
2. In a bowl combine all pie ingredients together and mix well
3. Pour the mixture over the pastry
4. Bake at 400-425 F for 25-30 minutes or until golden brown
5. When ready remove from the oven and let it rest for 15 minutes

CREAMSICLE SMOOTHIE

Serves: *1*

Prep Time: *5*   Minutes

Cook Time: *5*   Minutes

Total Time: *10*   Minutes

INGREDIENTS

- 2 cups mango
- 1 carrot
- 1 tablespoon apple cider vinegar
- 1 tsp lemon juice
- 1 cup coconut milk
- 1 tsp honey

DIRECTIONS

1. In a blender place all ingredients and blend until smooth
2. Pour smoothie in a glass and serve

BUTTERMILK SMOOTHIE

Serves: **1**

Prep Time: **5**   Minutes

Cook Time: **5**   Minutes

Total Time: **10**   Minutes

INGREDIENTS

- 1 cup strawberries
- 1 cup buttermilk
- 1 cup ice
- 1 tsp honey
- 1 tsp agave syrup

DIRECTIONS

1. In a blender place all ingredients and blend until smooth
2. Pour smoothie in a glass and serve

Serves: *1*
Prep Time: *5*   Minutes

Cook Time: *5*   Minutes

Total Time: *10*   Minutes

INGREDIENTS

- 1 banana
- 1 cup pineapple
- ¼ cup parsley
- 1 tsp chia seeds
- 1 cup ice

DIRECTIONS

1. **In a blender place all ingredients and blend until smooth**
2. **Pour smoothie in a glass and serve**

POMEGRANATE SMOOTHIE

Serves: **1**

Prep Time: **5** Minutes

Cook Time: **5** Minutes

Total Time: **10** Minutes

INGREDIENTS

- 1 cup pomegranate juice
- ¼ cup vanilla yogurt
- 3 cooked beets
- ¼ cup grapefruit juice
- 1 tablespoon honey
- 1 cup ice

DIRECTIONS

1. In a blender place all ingredients and blend until smooth
2. Pour smoothie in a glass and serve

CASHEW SMOOTHIE

Serves: *1*
Prep Time: *5*   Minutes

Cook Time: *5*   Minutes

Total Time: *10*   Minutes

INGREDIENTS

- 1 cup cashew milk
- 1 cup vanilla yogurt
- 1 banana
- 1 cup pumpkin puree
- 1 cup ice

DIRECTIONS

1. In a blender place all ingredients and blend until smooth
2. Pour smoothie in a glass and serve

PISTACHIOS ICE-CREAM

Serves: **6-8**

Prep Time: **15**   Minutes

Cook Time: **15**   Minutes

Total Time: **30**   Minutes

INGREDIENTS

- 4 egg yolks
- 1 cup heavy cream
- 1 cup milk
- 1 cup sugar
- 1 vanilla bean
- 1 tsp almond extract
- 1 cup cherries
- ½ cup pistachios

DIRECTIONS

1. In a saucepan whisk together all ingredients
2. Mix until bubbly
3. Strain into a bowl and cool
4. Whisk in favorite fruits and mix well
5. Cover and refrigerate for 2-3 hours

6. Pour mixture in the ice-cream maker and follow manufacturer instructions
7. Serve when ready

VANILLA ICE-CREAM

Serves: *6-8*

Prep Time: *15*   Minutes

Cook Time: *15*   Minutes

Total Time: *30*   Minutes

INGREDIENTS

- 1 cup milk
- 1 tablespoon cornstarch
- 1 oz. cream cheese
- 1 cup heavy cream
- 1 cup brown sugar
- 1 tablespoon corn syrup
- 1 vanilla bean

DIRECTIONS

8. In a saucepan whisk together all ingredients
9. Mix until bubbly
10. Strain into a bowl and cool
11. Whisk in favorite fruits and mix well
12. Cover and refrigerate for 2-3 hours
13. Pour mixture in the ice-cream maker and follow manufacturer instructions
14. Serve when ready

THANK YOU FOR READING THIS BOOK!